WINGED ENCOUNTERS

THE COMMON BIRDS OF DUBLIN

RAYMOND BEGGAN

WINGED ENCOUNTERS

THE COMMON BIRDS OF DUBLIN

THE LILLIPUT PRESS

DUBLIN

First published 2013 by

THE LILLIPUT PRESS LTD

62–63 Sitric Road, Arbour Hill, Dublin 7, Ireland
www.lilliputpress.ie

ISBN 978 1 84351 399 5

1 3 5 7 9 10 8 6 4 2

Set in 8.5 pt on 15 pt Sun Serif
Design by Niall McCormack
Printed and bound in Spain by GraphyCems

CONTENTS

PREFACE

THIS BOOK IS A COLLECTION of one hundred and twenty-one photographs, taken over the past two years, of the common birds seen daily in Dublin city and environs, along the banks of rivers and canals and in our public parks. They are for the most part larger and medium-sized birds, with the largest of them all, the mute swan, having the most entries. Swans are fascinating creatures and a joy and challenge to photograph. They are among the heaviest creatures on earth capable of flight.

I chose the title *Winged Encounters* because I didn't generally go out to shoot something specific; I came across these birds as they went about their daily struggle to survive. I have divided this book into three sections: 'Flight', 'Portraits' and 'Encounters'. I have tried to portray the lives of swans, herons, mallard, tufted and mandarin ducks, cormorants, different gull species and pigeons, with themed spreads throughout. The affection and goodwill of Dubliners for their birds is extraordinary, but the very existence of birds, and of wildlife in general, will always be greatly influenced by what we do, or don't do; in this, we have a duty of care. In that spirit I hope these pictures will inspire people to look again at the great treasure in the air that surrounds us.

RAYMOND BEGGAN

PART ONE

FLIGHT

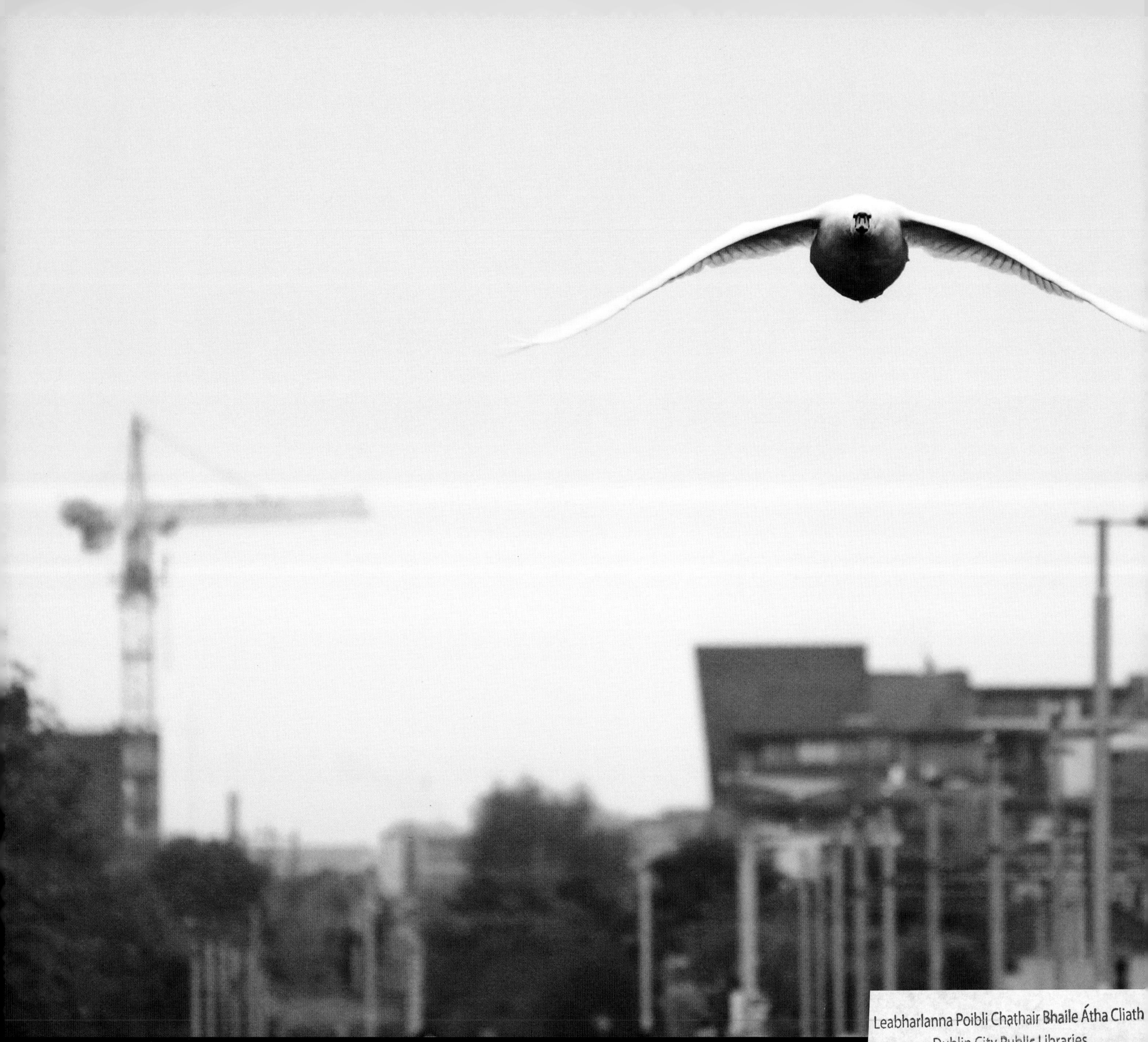

ABOVE: Parallel flying up the Grand Canal.

OPPOSITE: A swan races up the Liffey. Knockmaroon Hill, Chapelizod.

PREVIOUS PAGE: Eye in the sky, over Drimnagh Luas station footbridge.

ABOVE: On the bridge in St Stephen's Green I watched this young swan being bullied by an older male. He rose to escape and flew directly towards me. The swan realized it couldn't avoid the overhanging branches, wobbled and fell into the bush on the far side of the bridge. He seemed unhurt, but his tormentor awaited in the waters by the bank.

OPPOSITE: A pair of young swans land in a flourish of grace and beauty.

OVERLEAF: The drama, noise and churning of a mass take-off. The Grand Canal, Portobello.

ABOVE: A leisurely 'Spruce Goose' landing. Harold's Cross Bridge.

OPPOSITE: The intensity, bulk and power of a large adult male swan in the heave for momentum. The Liffey, Knockmaroon Hill.

OVERLEAF: A young swan roars down the canal towards La Touche Bridge, Portobello.

ABOVE: The large, versatile webbed feet of the mute swan are powerful paddles, air
and water breaks, and the moving pendulums used to balance on land.

OPPOSITE: Portobello Harbour is a familiar home to many Dublin city-centre swans.
Locals create daily feeding frenzies with the ghosts of their bread bins.

ABOVE: Seagulls dance in the sky, moving in any direction, on any axis. A swan's flight evokes jumbo jets, a seagull's helicopters. St Stephen's Green.

OPPOSITE: Diving for food. Malahide Estuary.

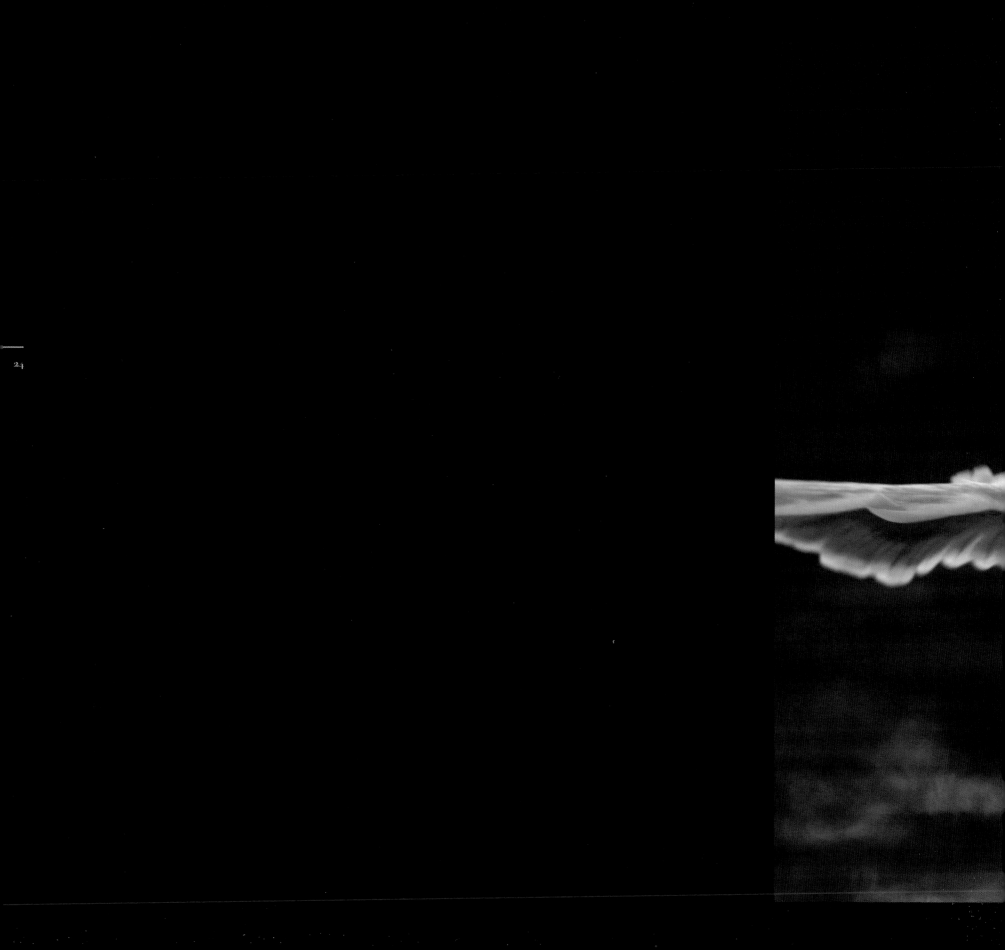

The grey heron famously waits at the water's edge for long periods, totally still, catching its prey with swift precision in its sharp beak. Often appearing smaller than it is, its body acts like an accordion. Its distinctive call resonates across the water. This particular heron is a familiar sight in Tymon Park, Tallaght. It competes more successfully than other birds for the bread on offer.

ABOVE: Gliding over sea water. A heron just offshore at Irishtown Nature Park.

OPPOSITE: A heron with a pinkeen in its beak, flying down the canal. It had just eaten a duckling ten minutes before. Rialto.

Cormorants fly as if, in stopping for a second, they would fall from the sky. This extraordinary creature lives equally under water, on land and in the air.

OPPOSITE: Cormorants seem to prefer flying over water.

OVERLEAF: A startled cormorant shoots down the Liffey.

A startled flock takes to the air in a flurry. Pigeons happily live off the food we discard. These beautiful birds find no love in some quarters; I once knew a girl who kept small stones in her bag as a defence against them.

OVERLEAF: Pigeons flying into a sunlit passage. The Grand Canal, Windsor Terrace.

Ducks almost seem to enjoy flying. The daring chases, their squabbles and social behaviour, all convey a youthful energy. Male mallards spend a lot of time chasing, and tormenting, female ducks.

OPPOSITE: A mallard duck changes direction mid-flight, eyeing the camera

OVERLEAF: Female mallards in flight. Bushy Park, Terenure.

Swans often appear to act independently or in pairs, but sometimes they spring
into collective action. La Touche Bridge, Portobello.

PART TWO

PORTRAITS

ABOVE: Framed by a rainbow, swans, geese and seagulls battle for food as
smaller birds are left with crumbs. Bray Harbour, Co. Wicklow.

ABOVE: The heron is like an actor who dons many costumes.
'Play it, Sam.' Blessington Street Basin.

OPPOSITE: A knight in armour looks on. Blessington Street Basin.

OVERLEAF: The chorus line. Swans in sync as a heron takes centre
stage. Irish National War Memorial Gardens, Islandbridge.

ABOVE: A duck's-eye view of ducks.

RIGHT: Ducks on a wall. Martin's Row, Chapelizod.

OPPOSITE: A female duck perching on a piece of wood
as rain starts to fall. Ranelagh Gardens.

RIGHT: When their feathers are wet, cormorants look as if they have been pulled out of a black oil slick.

BELOW RIGHT: When their feathers dry out, they appear like statues carved from wood.

BELOW LEFT: A cormorant surfacing under Harold's Cross Bridge.

OPPOSITE: Classic pose. A cormorant, wings outstretched, absorbing heat from the sun. Lakelands, Terenure College.

ABOVE: A swan flies under the bridge at Drimnagh Luas station.

OPPOSITE: Conducting a ghoulish orchestra, a cormorant rises
from the deep. Blessington Street Basin.

OVERLEAF: The many faces of the mute swan.

Tufted ducks landing awkwardly on the ice.
Blessington Street Basin.

OPPOSITE: A mandarin duck drake feels
the freezing winds rustle his mane.
Blessington Street Basin.

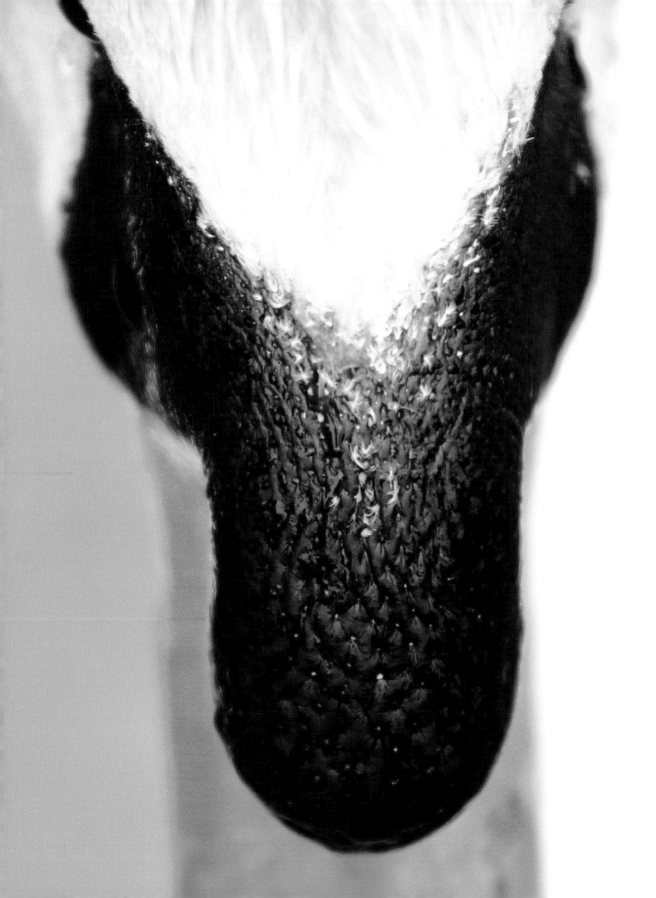

ABOVE: A heron wearing an outfit of reed, just below Dolphin's Barn Bridge.

OPPOSITE: Camouflaged in Tymon Park.

Daily rituals. Cleaning, preening and wing inspections.

Dogs, illnesses and scrapping are some of the reasons a swan may lose its feathers. Swans rarely back out of a fight and can be unbelievably aggressive when riled.

OPPOSITE: Male ducks are often fighting and biting each other. This drake has a scarred head and neck.

The birds we meet in public spaces come to rely on humans to feed them; they learn to be quick on the draw and nimble of beak. Young swans who stay with their parents too long into the mating season can be subject to brutal treatment. These birds are often brought out by rescuers to Malahide Estuary and resettled there.

REVERIE I

LEFT: A focal point in the surroundings.
Lakelands, Terenure College.

OPPOSITE: A cormorant resting on the
branch of a tree. The Liffey, Chapelizod.

REVERIE II

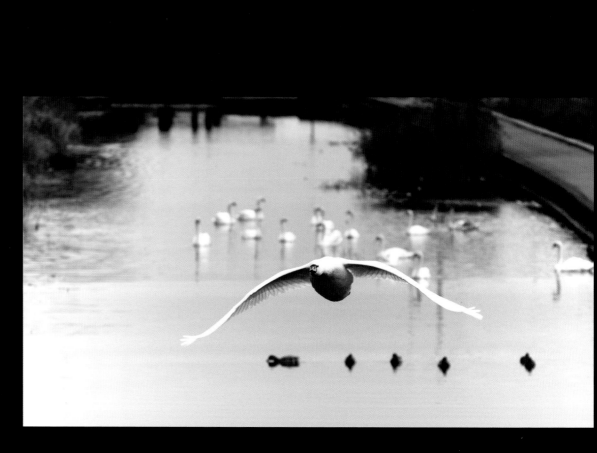

REVERIE III

Swans departing.

REVERIE IV

ABOVE: A blackbird in a plum tree. Chapelizod.

OPPOSITE: A swan embracing the morning. The Grand Canal, Portobello.

ABOVE: A fluffy moor hen chick explores the Grand Canal.

LEFT: A cygnet tucked up in the wings of its mother on the Liffey.

OPPOSITE: Ducklings are very vulnerable; many don't survive long enough to take to the sky.

OPPOSITE: The crew members in this rowing boat don't realize just how close a thirty-pound bird travelling at 40 mph has come to colliding with them.

Because of their size and sometimes aggressive temperament, people have mixed reactions to swans. Some speed up when walking past them, while others are spellbound and want to get closer.

It is a long way from the world of the Children of Lir to the concrete, traffic-filled city centre of today. Swans bridge these worlds, bringing the mythical and glorious to the urbane and commonplace. Encountering wildlife and having access to nature makes life bearable for many people living within these confines.

Winnie acting all brave from the comfort of our home on the raised bank of the Liffey. Sometimes swans come into the garden. Winnie is nowhere to be seen.

There comes a point when birds will look the
photographer straight in the eye.

OPPOSITE: A cormorant up close.

LEFT: A swan and a cormorant almost form a love heart with their necks.

BELOW: A young girl with colourful runners leaps over the sand in Bray Harbour.

OPPOSITE: By air, land and water. Goldenbridge Lock.

OVERLEAF: Two swans align to create a four-winged creature.

ABOVE: To other birds, even to small dogs, swans must seem enormous.

OPPOSITE: A mandarin duck preening on the top of the waterfall by
Dodder Road Lower. This bird is a new sight in Dublin.

ABOVE: There is something amiss with people who mindlessly discard things in our rivers and canals.

OPPOSITE: The riverbank at Bushy Park. Dublin's public parks are to be cherished.

OVERLEAF: A heron sails down the Dodder. Dodder Road Lower.

FINAL SPREAD: An encounter while lying on the bottom of a canoe, camera in hand. A large male swan charges. He was a regular visitor to our house, where we fed him scraps and oats. I was desperately hoping he would recognize me as he advanced and become less threatening. He did.

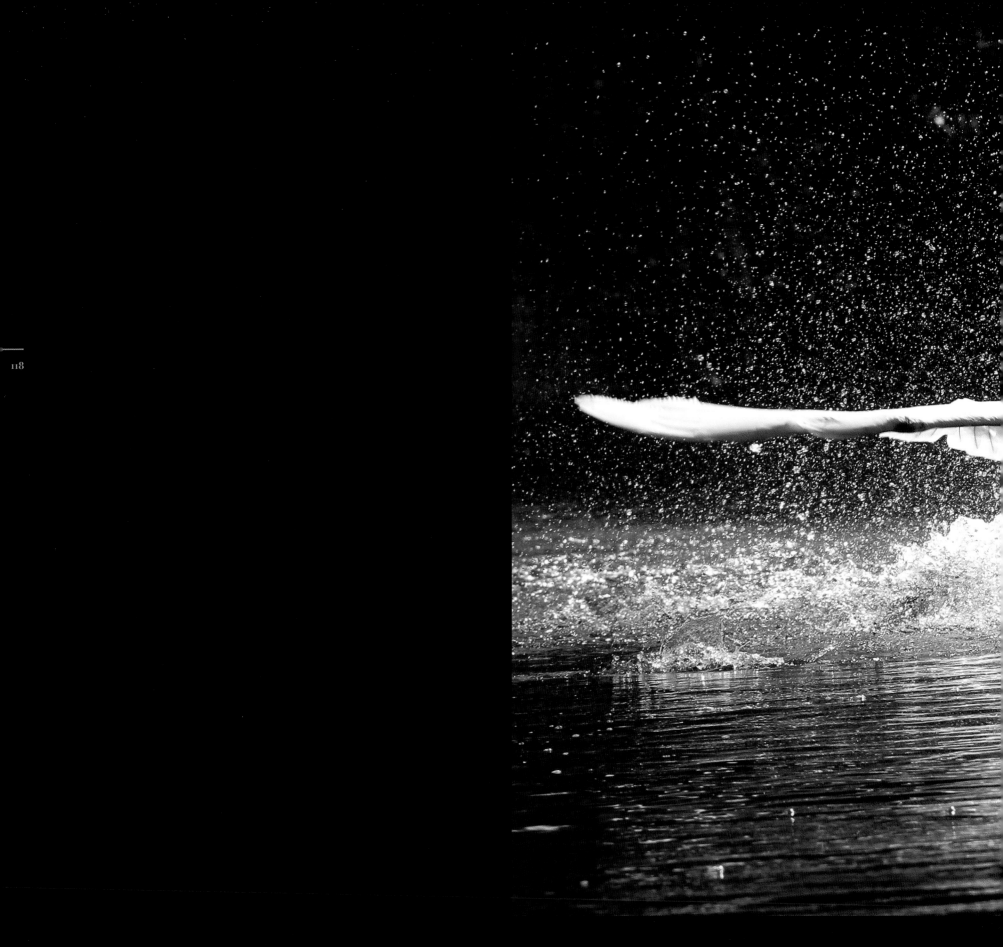

TECHNICAL NOTES

PAGES 2-3. Canon 7D, Canon 70-200 f4 IS, 1/800, f/4.0, ISO 250
PAGE 4. Canon 7D, Sigma 70-200 f2.8, 1/1250, f/5.6, ISO 200
PAGE 5. Canon 7D, Sigma 70-200 f2.8, 1/1000, f/3.2, ISO 1000
PAGES 6-7. Canon 7D, Canon 70-200 f4 IS, 1/1600, f/8.0, ISO 640
PAGE 8. Canon 600D, Canon 70-200 f4 IS, 1/800, f/14, ISO 800
PAGE 9. Canon 7D, Sigma 70-200 f2.8, 1/1250, f/4.5, ISO 500
PAGES 10-11. Canon 7D, Canon 70-200 f4 IS, 1/1600, f/8.0, ISO 640
PAGE 12. Canon 7D, Canon 70-200 f4 IS, 1/1000, f/9.0, ISO 640
PAGE 13. Canon 7D, Canon 70-200 f4 IS, 1/800, f/8.0, ISO 320
PAGES 14-15. Canon 7D, Sigma 70-200 f2.8, 1/1250, f/5.6, ISO 500
PAGE 16. Canon 7D, Canon 70-200 f4 IS, 1/1000, f/8.0, ISO 400
PAGE 17. Canon 7D, Sigma 70-200 f2.8, 1/1250, f/4.5, ISO 200
PAGE 18-19. Canon 7D, Canon 70-200 f4 IS, 1/2500, f/8.0, ISO 400
PAGE 20. Canon 7D, Sigma 18-50 f2.8 DC, 1/2000, f/2.8, ISO 320
PAGE 21. Canon 7D, Canon 70-200 f4 IS, 1/1250, f/8.0, ISO 320
PAGES 22-23. Canon 7D, Sigma 400 f5.6, 1/1600, f/5.6, ISO 640
PAGES 24-25. Canon 7D, Sigma 70-200 f2.8, 1/1000, f/4.0, ISO 400
PAGE 26. Canon 7D, Canon 70-200 f4 IS, 1/1250, f/9.0, ISO 400
PAGE 27. Canon 600D, Canon 70-200 f4 IS, 1/1000, f/11, ISO 640
PAGE 28. Canon 7D, Canon 70-200 f4 IS, 1/1000, f/10.0, ISO 400
PAGE 29 TOP. Canon 7D, Canon 70-200 f4 IS, 1/1000, f/7.1, ISO 400
PAGE 29 BOTTOM. Canon 7D, Canon 70-200 f4 IS, 1/1000, f/4.0, ISO 320
PAGE 30. Canon 7D, Sigma 400 f5.6, 1/2500, f/5.6, ISO 400
PAGE 31. Canon 7D, Sigma 70-200 f2.8, 1/1000, f/6.3, ISO 500
PAGE 32. Canon 7D, Sigma 70-200 f2.8, 1/1000, f/3.5, ISO 200
PAGE 33. Canon 7D, Sigma 70-200 f2.8, 1/500, f/5.0, ISO 500
PAGE 34 LEFT. Canon 7D, Canon 70-200 f4 IS, 1/800, f/4.0, ISO 1000
PAGE 34 RIGHT. Canon 7D, Sigma 70-200 f2.8, 1/640, f/6.3, ISO 100
PAGE 35. Canon 7D, Canon 70-200 f4 IS, 1/1250, f/5.6, ISO 1250
PAGES 36-37. Canon 7D, Canon 70-200 f4 IS, 1/1000, f/6.3, ISO 2000
PAGE 38. Canon 7D, Sigma 18-50 f2.8 DC, 1/1600, f/2.8, ISO 500
PAGE 39. Canon 7D, Canon 70-200 f4 IS, 1/1600, f/4.5, ISO 320
PAGE 40. Canon 7D, Canon 70-200 f4 IS, 1/1000, f/7.1, ISO 400
PAGE 41. Canon 7D, Canon 70-200 f4 IS, 1/800, f/7.1, ISO 400
PAGE 42 TOP. Canon 7D, Sigma 70-200 f2.8, 1/1600, f/5.6, ISO 1600
PAGE 42 BOTTOM. Canon 7D, Sigma 400 f5.6, 1/2500, f/5.6, ISO 800
PAGE 43. Canon 7D, Sigma 70-200 f2.8, 1/1000, f/4.5, ISO 1000
PAGE 44. Canon 7D, Canon 70-200 f4 IS, 1/1000, f/4.0, ISO 1600
PAGE 45. Canon 7D, Canon 70-200 f4 IS, 1/1000, f/4.0, ISO 800
PAGE 46. Canon 7D, Canon 70-200 f4 IS, 1/1600, f/8.0, ISO 320

PAGE 47. Canon 7D, Sigma 400 f5.6, 1/500, f/5.6, ISO 320
PAGE 48. Canon 7D, Canon 70-200 f4 IS, 1/100, f/6.3, ISO 320
PAGE 49. Canon 7D, Sigma 18-50 f2.8 DC, 1/2000, f/8.0, ISO 100
PAGE 52. Canon 7D, Sigma 18-50 f2.8 DC, 1/320, f/16.0, ISO 320
PAGE 53. Canon 7D, Sigma 70-200 f2.8, 1/640, f/5.6, ISO 500
PAGES 54-55. Canon 7D, Sigma 18-50 f2.8 DC, 1/400, f/10.0, ISO 200
PAGE 56. Canon 7D, Sigma 400 f5.6, 1/1000, f/5.6, ISO 200
PAGE 57. Canon 7D, Sigma 70-200 f2.8, 1/400, f/5.0, ISO 200
PAGES 58-59. Canon 7D, Sigma 400 f5.6, 1/800, f/5.6, ISO 500
PAGE 60. Canon 7D, Sigma 70-200 f2.8, 1/400, f/5.0, ISO 200
PAGE 61 TOP. Canon 7D, Sigma 18-50 f2.8 DC, 1/125, f/5.6, ISO 100
PAGE 61 BOTTOM. Canon 7D, Canon 70-200 f4 IS, 1/320, f/4.0, ISO 500
PAGE 62. Canon 7D, Sigma 70-200 f2.8, 1/1250, f/5.6, ISO 320
PAGE 63 BOTTOM L. Canon 7D, Sigma 70-200 f2.8, 1/1000, f/5.0, ISO 800
PAGE 63 BOTTOM R. Canon 7D, Sigma 70-200 f2.8, 1/1250, f/5.6, ISO 320
PAGE 63 TOP. Canon 7D, Canon 70-300 f4-5.6 IS, 1/200, f/5.0, ISO 400
PAGE 64. Canon 7D, Canon 70-200 f4 IS, 1/1250, f/7.1, ISO 500
PAGE 65. Canon 7D, Canon 70-200 f4 IS, 1/400, f/8.0, ISO 400
PAGE 66 TOP. Canon 7D, Sigma 18-50 f2.8 DC, 1/4000, f/4.5, ISO 400
PAGE 66 BOTTOM. Canon 7D, Sigma 18-50 f2.8 DC, 1/1000, f/4.5, ISO 200
PAGE 67. Canon 7D, Sigma 18-50 f2.8 DC, 1/250, f/4.5, ISO 800
PAGE 68 TOP. Canon 7D, Sigma 70-200 f2.8, 1/1000, f/4.0, ISO 1250
PAGE 68 BOTTOM. Canon 7D, Sigma 70-200 f2.8, 1/1000, f/5.6, ISO 800
PAGE 69. Canon 7D, Sigma 70-200 f2.8, 1/1000, f/5.6, ISO 800
PAGE 70. Canon 7D, Canon 70-200 f4 IS, 1/1000, f/5.0, ISO 320
PAGE 71. Canon 600D, Canon 70-200 f4 IS, 1/800, f/5.6, ISO 200
PAGE 72. Canon 7D, Sigma 400 f5.6, 1/1000, f/5.6, ISO 640
PAGE 73. Canon 7D, Canon 70-200 f4 IS, 1/1250, f/4.0, ISO 640
PAGE 74. Canon 7D, Canon 70-200 f4 IS, 1/1000, f/7.1, ISO 320
PAGE 75. Canon 600D, Canon 70-200 f4 IS, 1/1000, f/6.3, ISO 320
PAGE 76 TOP. Canon 7D, Sigma 70-200 f2.8, 1/1250, f/5.6, ISO 640
PAGE 76 BOTTOM L. Canon 7D, Sigma 400 f5.6, 1/800, f/5.6, ISO 500
PAGE 76 BOTTOM R. Canon 7D, Sigma 400 f5.6, 1/2000, f/5.6, ISO 400
PAGE 77. Canon 7D, Sigma 400 f5.6, 1/1000, f/5.6, ISO 1000
PAGE 78 TOP. Canon 7D, Sigma 70-200 f2.8, 1/1600, f/7.1, ISO 320
PAGE 78 BOTTOM. Canon 7D, Sigma 70-200 f2.8, 1/1600, f/5.6, ISO 400
PAGE 79. Canon 7D, Canon 70-200 f4 IS, 1/400, f/5.0, ISO 400
PAGE 80 TOP. Canon 600D, Canon 70-200 f4 IS, 1/640, f/8.0, ISO 320
PAGE 80 BOTTOM. Canon 7D, Canon 70-200 f4 IS, 1/1000, f/4.0, ISO 400
PAGE 81. Canon 7D, Canon 70-200 f4 IS, 1/1000, f/9.0, ISO 400

PAGE 82. Canon 7D, Sigma 18-50 f2.8 DC, 1/320, f/9.0, ISO 400
PAGE 83. Canon 7D, Canon 70-200 f4 IS, 1/200, f/4.0, ISO 1250
PAGE 84. Canon 7D, Sigma 400 f5.6, 1/1000, f/5.6, ISO 320
PAGE 85. Canon 7D, Canon 70-200 f4 IS, 1/800, f/9.0, ISO 500
PAGE 86 LEFT. Canon 7D, Canon 70-200 f4 IS, 1/1250, f/5.6, ISO 320
PAGE 86 RIGHT. Canon 7D, Canon 70-200 f4 IS, 1/800, f/4.0, ISO 250
PAGE 87. Canon 7D, Sigma 18-50 f2.8 DC, 1/400, f/2.8, ISO 800
PAGE 88. Canon 7D, Sigma 70-200 f2.8, 1/1000, f/3.2, ISO 200
PAGE 89. Canon 7D, Sigma 400 f5.6, 1/2000, f/5.6, ISO 400
PAGE 90 TOP. Canon 7D, Sigma 70-200 f2.8, 1/1250, f/9.0, ISO 640
PAGE 90 BOTTOM. Canon 7D, Sigma 70-200 f2.8, 1/1000, f/5.6, ISO 200
PAGE 91. Canon 7D, Canon 70-200 f4 IS, 1/1000, f/5.6, ISO 200
PAGE 94 TOP. Canon 7D, Sigma 18-50 f2.8 DC, 1/1600, f/2.8, ISO 640
PAGE 94 BOTTOM. Canon 7D, Sigma 400 f5.6, 1/1600, f/5.6, ISO 500
PAGE 95. Canon 7D, Sigma 70-200 f2.8, 1/1250, f/3.5, ISO 200
PAGE 96. Canon 7D, Sigma 70-200 f2.8, 1/1600, f/5.6, ISO 3200
PAGE 97 TOP. Canon 7D, Sigma 70-200 f2.8, 1/1600, f/5.6, ISO 400
PAGE 97 BOTTOM. Canon 600D, Canon 70-200 f4 IS, 1/800, f/8.0, ISO 320
PAGE 98. Canon 600D, Canon 70-200 f4 IS, 1/640, f/4.0, ISO 640
PAGE 99. Canon 7D, Sigma 400 f5.6, 1/1600, f/5.6, ISO 320
PAGE 100. Canon 7D, Sigma 18-50 f2.8 DC, 1/80, f/4.0, ISO 100
PAGE 101. Canon 7D, Sigma 70-200 f2.8, 1/1250, f/5.0, ISO 800
PAGE 102 LEFT. Canon 7D, Canon 70-200 f4 IS, 1/800, f/8.0, ISO 400
PAGE 102 RIGHT. Canon 7D, Sigma 18-50 f2.8 DC, 1/200, f/8.0, ISO 250
PAGE 103. Canon 7D, Canon 70-200 f4 IS, 1/1000, f/8.0, ISO 400
PAGE 104. Canon 7D, Canon 70-300 f4-5.6 IS, 1/250, f/5.6, ISO 160
PAGE 105 TOP. Canon 7D, Sigma 400 f5.6, 1/1000, f/5.6, ISO 500
PAGE 105 BOTTOM. Canon 7D, Sigma 70-200 f2.8, 1/1000, f/2.8, ISO 160
PAGE 106 TOP. Canon 7D, Canon 70-300 f4-5.6 IS, 1/600, f/5.6, ISO 1000
PAGE 106 BOTTOM. Canon 7D, Sigma 18-50 f2.8 DC, 1/2000, f/7.1, ISO 400
PAGE 107. Canon 7D, Canon 70-200 f4 IS, 1/800, f/4.5, ISO 640
PAGES 108-109. Canon 7D, Sigma 70-200 f2.8, 1/1250, f/5.6, ISO 400
PAGE 110. Canon 7D, Sigma 18-50 f2.8 DC, 1/1250, f/5.6, ISO 320
PAGE 111. Canon 7D, Sigma 18-50 f2.8 DC, 1/800, f/10.0, ISO 200
PAGE 112. Canon 7D, Sigma 18-50 f2.8 DC, 1/6400, f/3.2, ISO 200
PAGE 113. Canon 600D, Canon 70-200 f4 IS, 1/1000, f/4.0, ISO 640
PAGE 114. Canon 7D, Sigma 18-50 f2.8 DC, 1/200, f/5.0, ISO 100
PAGE 115. Canon 7D, Canon 50 f1.8, 1/50, f/1.8, ISO 800
PAGES 116-117. Canon 7D, Canon 70-200 f4 IS, 1/1600, f/8.0, ISO 160
PAGES 118-119. Canon 7D, Canon 70-200 f4 IS, 1/800, f/10.0, ISO 320

I used Digital Photo Professional and Photoshop when needed to crop photographs, adjust brightness and contrast, and occasionally to sharpen and/or convert images to black and white. Some photos have a vignette effect added.